CARNAL LOVE

Poems

Henri Deluy

*

*Translated from the French
by Guy Bennett*

*pour
Kristin
de tés loin
et de trés
près*

SUN &
MOON

CLASSICS

121

LOS ANGELES
SUN & MOON PRESS
1996

CARNAL LOVE

Sun & Moon Press
A Program of The Contemporary Arts Educational Project, Inc.
a nonprofit corporation
6026 Wilshire Boulevard, Los Angeles, California 90036

This edition first published in 1996 by Sun & Moon Press
10 9 8 7 6 5 4 3 2 1
FIRST ENGLISH LANGUAGE EDITION 1996

This book was made possible, in part, through an operational grant from the
Andrew W. Mellon Foundation and through contributions to
The Contemporary Arts Educational Project. Inc.,
a nonprofit corporation

Cover: Katie Messborn, *Black Cherries* [based on a painting,
Embracing a Red Landscape (1994) by Ofelia Rodriguez]
Design: Katie Messborn
Typography: Guy Bennett

LIBRARY OF CONGRESS CATALOGING IN PUBLICATION DATA
Deluy, Henri [1931]
Carnal Love
p. cm—(Sun & Moon Classics: 121)
ISBN: 1-55713-272-0
I. Title. II. Series III. Translator
811' .54 dc20

Printed in the United States of America on acid-free paper.

CONTENTS

"If you've skimped on effort in the pale, early morning, you'll get nailed in the cruel spotlight."

— JOE FRAZIER
World Heavyweight Champion

AN (ENIGMATIC) GRAMMAR

Because there was the Portrait, there were,
That year, a lot of poppies,
And black cherries.

*

You weren't. – You were prose.
Because prose was there, birds,
Always a lot of birds, a lot
More birds, mornings, evenings.
An (enigmatic) grammar.

*

Prose was then, for a time,
The prose of the world: because there was
Prose, the earth turned again, for a while,
Black.

*

Yes.

Your hand was black. – It wrote.
It formed, in the sun, little signs.
A froth, in search of a wide open face
(Or another face.)

*

You made bouquets, with flowers,
Long stems, grasses, tall grasses,
Branches. – You burned them. Your mouth
Became crimson. Your phantom touched
Another phantom. – You turned
From the observation of shadows.

Always, we exchanged conventional
And cordial words. – You tried,
It wasn't another lie, you said,
(In spite of this world of symbols, the interminable
Discrepancies of memory and immediate
Indifference), to say that the poem was
A simple thing and not the slow
Extremes of affective urgency; of
An astonishment that would come
From the chain of words.

*

The poem could be satisfied with one night:
We knew it.

A few December roses, still,
Roses, real roses, with little fragrance,
All petals, heavy, satiny petals.
It was important not to stop talking. For
The poem was still the poem, for
You couldn't do anything else
With your body.

Talk about the night. – About the tips
Of your fingers. – To walk down to the steep
Slope surrounding the house. To run
To the water's edge (the water, here, was
The sea); no longer to see your upper thighs,
nor mine. – Nor Stalin's Portrait.

Later, in Moscow, capital, I kept,
For the first time, a travel
Diary. – Nearby, before the churches,
Rooks, more and more of them,
Flocked together. – I still wasn't
Dreaming. I wanted to be sure I
Wasn't dreaming. I was happy, here, that
My father was dead.

Not to believe. – Not to end up in the hospital.
Because anxiety was still
The best thing there was. Because
Anxiety, for the moment, coincided
With these flowers, at best, before our eyes,
On the ground, in a bucket filled with water,
A blue metal bucket, between the rug and the table.

*

The dream was terribly fragile,
Your dream.

The sun was up. It had crossed
The mass of water-swollen trees. – Nothing
Happened in that light, that morning.

*

A gladiola, hardly ruffled, resisted.
The eyes lost themselves in the curtain
Of trees. Hoar frost, under the corolla
Of a flower. It was very cold.

*

First gestures, and death settled in
To half the body.

In the garden, after the Kremlin,
(A next-to-last visit), a small,
Long-tailed bird, was as elegant as an oriole.

*

It was an ordinary dream. – To know
What it was. – The dream only existed
In the dream. He began to think.
The dream was a pure diversion.

Years later, in Cairo, on the Nile,
Doves occupied a pigeonry,
On the terrace roof, camels
Lifted their heads, while winter
Composed a long-past pattern.

*

A little boy stood near
A wooden boat.

To say: I liked the green stem of the plants; to say:
I liked the colorful tigers, the illustrated
Chronologies, the inaccessible realities, the invisible
Structures of emotion, and, also, sudden sadness,
A bit abrupt, which subdued the charm of the narrative which,
However, came from the writing.

What I said. – I did not say it all.
The word that I didn't say, you didn't want
Me to say it. – The word of the night.
It became even more remote;
With the fragrance of the body that evoked it,
And, nearby, what remained
Red in the blue of the sky.

*

Then falling back,
You said: no more politics.

Something which allowed the discovery
Of little truths. – The tiny undulations
Of the sea, and threads, hanging
Into water. – You were alone, to contemplate
The softness, and this thin line, hardly
Moving. – Without a shadow.

Your body was immortal. – I told you
Your body was immortal. I told you
It was insignificant. And
Most often, you walked,
Not far from the city.

It was a smile without conviction, almost
Reluctant. – To accept it, as such.
In the foggy night. With a cold wind.
Then, to leave the spot. To find yourself again
In the middle of the street.

An exaggerated individualism, a vigilant law,
A moral code: he liked idealized sexual
Objects, or plain old smut. – He had
Just been admitted to the hospital: a broken nose,
Two fractured ribs, broken fingers,
A cracked wrist, shattered jaw.

Flesh, that's what we said:
Flesh. – So as not to say.
And blood, that we spoke of at night.

*

With skin in a suitcase and the suitcase
    In a hotel room
With this music that appeared to be
    An Egyptian tree.

July was no longer July and did not come back.
All we could see now were the tree tops.
There was, in this rejection of vain hopes,
Of overly intimate passions, a mental ruse
That attempted to shut off its own logic;
And now the absence of leaves was
The mark of winter; that a light emphasis
Allowed to exaggerate all.
So this anxiety arose from a problem
That came from no one.

The acanthus coiled around
    The stone lion.
The eye was purple. – Airplane noise
    In the gardens, in Rome,
Above the Piazza del Popolo.

*

Further away, down below, on a well-to-do building,
    The old plaque,
Emphasizing Joyce's memory gave
    Another meaning to the narrative.

To emerge a moment into the deep ochres,
    Yellows, reds,
The browns marked, with clay
    Dust on the façades.

*

May hell give the muscles of a burned tongue
    Its infinite suppleness,
        You said.

To say: I liked the ashen color
    Of dried flowers,
The broken white, the black, the gray;
    To say: I liked
Nightfall, the shadow of shadows,
    And the obstinate work
        Of corruption.

*

To say: I like this work, the blue
    Color of the trunks of cherry trees
And the simple, or even unsavory
    Histories.

Broken colors of the mouth.
Veins of the wrists. – A thing
So violent it was suspended
In its very apparition. – You shrugged
Your shoulders, I took your hips.

Effects of the night. – Things
From the body. – Disciplines
Of love. – Don't touch my breasts,
You said, for a long time.

*

For the body had what it needed
To lie, to lie for a long time.

Something even more difficult;
What had just disappeared, an even more
Difficult thing. – You didn't come
Even when you said you were going to come,
You didn't come. Even when you said
You would come, you didn't come. And,
When you said you wouldn't come,
I had no reason to wait for
You to come, because you had said
You wouldn't come.

Because there was, on the Portrait, a reflection
Of this browned photo,
You told of its tender heart.
You said: as long as this reflection remains.

*

You did not want to find your face
Disfigured by strange adversities
That we had wished for.

At times the camaraderie was exemplary.

We saw the sea or we didn't.
We didn't see it. – Hardly did a mound
Of earth fill the landscape. – You were afraid
To believe what you could have said about yourself.

*

I hadn't seen the sea for a long time.
Hadn't seen it. – We didn't see
It.

Illimitable object of a fascination, the sea,
The sea remained suspended. – Not to blur
The image. – Not to take advantage of the poem.

*

Under the blue sky, the sky was black.
The end of a certainty. – The hum
Of the poem. – The flight into style.

Because there was this reflection, to dig
Into the shadow of the apple trees again,
To observe the out-stretched wing of a swallow;
To cross the night as it crosses the city.
To weather the wear. – The trees that withdrew
From the sea. – Your own image, covered with ash,
And the wolves that you observed, from the top of your hill.

*

Because there was a funny smell.

Since we hardly ever said
Anything about smells
In poems. – Even in times of misfortune
And need, and it was still of little significance,
you thought.

The young boy had crossed his arms,
High up. – He looked away,
In search of a memory. Way
To say: this is none of my business.

To receive the first love letter.

The mother was absent. The mother
Was rejected. – Time was needed
To multiply the traces, even the fugitive ones,
Of feeling, and its commentary. The sky
Took on a gray tint that told of
Fog. It was cold.

We had to note the expenses of writing.
See the light, beneath the bushes, pick up
The pieces. Move the question of verse.
Modify the break. Abridge the humor.
See the shadow when it moved
Toward the shadow of the bushes, the late arrival
Of frost, the folded earth, the arrangement
Of the true, the arrangement of the false.
Not to be mistaken. We weren't supposed
To talk too much on the shore.

Only the pomegranate flower kept,
From morning to evening, the same vividness, a bright
Red. – The landscape was sparse. – On the ground,
The earth thickened.

*

A few meters away, a young couple
Stopped, hesitated, walked along a wall,
Then set off again holding hands.

Autumn. – The trees, which seemed
So close; it was to autumn that the trees
Seemed closest to one another.
Not to believe it truly easier
To dream; or to flee.

Since there was the persistent scent
Of sage, the city was filthy.
Concern wore thin.
There was the Portrait. There was
A kindness in you, and this was
A quality that escaped me.

The sky was low. – It was still night.
This violence from you, against your own rage,
Too. Elsewhere, and not the scream. To want you, there,
In speculation, eager to say, in speech,
Then in word. – And, at times, your absence
Cut me in two.

With the lip, the tongue, the tips
Of the teeth, slowly crossing, without
Stop, the stomach, the silky softness.
To taste the warm, acrid humidity.
To let myself be straddled, to help myself with my hand.

IN TRUTH, IT WAS PROSE

To break the chain of words. – To break the sequence
Of words. – To break what the words thought they said
About the sequence of words. – To break what the chain
Added to the chain of words. – To break what the word
Thought it said about the truth of the chain of words.
To break what the word thought it said about its own truth.
To take the words one by one, not in solitude:
In isolation. Writing not to write anymore.

In spite of the persistent trace of blood and scraps of linen,
In spite of the rubbing of hands and the chaste unobtrusiveness,
Not to listen to the roar, to take anything away,
To ask any questions, to say no. – And then to speak, shortly
Afterwards,
In this official language, articulated carefully,
Cautious, precise, stripped of all intuitive
Subjectivity for fear of being too obvious. – Silently
To gather the scrupulous material of a few unfortunate
Words.

To close the eyes. – The night was covered
With down. – The night was buried in
Willow down. – The night,
Hung out to dry. – On the banks of the Tiber,
Was one of the two women my mother?

Prose was not what you said.
The horror of large mirrors, you said,
Since I met that somber girl,
Dressed in black, with her intensity,
A tremor, not at all erotic.
The city was filthy. – Rarely at night,
She said.

The city was filthy. – The truth was
Prose. Your fable was the right one.

*

I wish the flames of retribution
For the poem that cannot tell
What prose tells. – I like
To sleep in a bedroom whose curtains
Are not veiled. – That's what you said.

The truth no longer needed to be said.
She closed her eyes. Not to come back to it.
The sea was filthy. – The city too. The truth
Was a rumor. Not to play on the flashes.
Not to see anything.

*

It was cold. It was dark.
February's late snow, shoveled
In heaps along the brick walls
Was soiled, covered with a fine
Film of soot.

Because the evidence was there, nearby,
It remained foreign to memory.
The draft of a secret shared
Accumulated: to be able to feed
On this type of passion for a long time.

*

For he who knows blood. – To know
Blood. – The inability to take from the dream
What you were unaware of. – To be able to cry,
To be able to take out a little knife with a horn
Handle, to bow one's head.

The horizon was out of view. Sex
Dropped out of sight. Winter turned
Red. Birds turned round
The red of winter. Sex was
Ornamental…. That pleasure was
A muscular pleasure.

*

It was not a lie. You could
Have made a gesture.

To tell the truth among the unknown
Fragments of unknown words. Not
To come back to it. Not to get anything out of it
Other than the risk of loving. A little knife
With a horn handle. And blue magpies.

You aren't telling the truth. If you knew the truth
You wouldn't say it. You aren't saying anything about the truth.
If you knew a fragment of the truth, you wouldn't
Say it. You add nothing to the truth. If you didn't
Know the truth, you wouldn't say it. You say
Nothing about the truth. You add nothing to the lie.
You say nothing about the lie. You walk quickly.
The sun swings back to its zenith.
Lying to lie, you said.

To plunge back into memories.
To let ourselves be lead through familiar
Objects. Sex: an instrument.

*

To prepare ourselves to think like this.
To prepare ourselves to talk about
Love. To prepare ourselves to need
Flowers, and a red dress.

To paste up the first posters.

The bedroom seemed to emerge from the body.
The bedroom seemed to emerge from the folds
Of the robe and the folds of the body.
The bedroom seemed to receive
Something else as well. – You said:
When I leave, I will go far away
And without any regrets. – The bedroom was
Altogether in this confused heap
Of words, next to the dress, and
In this landscape, that disappears
Toward your upper thighs.

You didn't make up what you knew.
You caught on quickly to the words
Of the foreign language. – The make-up.
The outsides of intimacy, the discretion,
For the story was incredible – in which nearly
Everything remained to be done – it was true.

Near the Portrait, the landscape was sparse.

*

I didn't know what apathy was any more.

I didn't know what you had told me.
I didn't know what you hadn't told me.
I didn't know why you hadn't told me,
I didn't know why you had decided
To say it. I didn't know why now.
Now, I didn't know what you were going to say.
I didn't know your question.

For a long time in his nightly fantasies
He had acted like this, with this detachment,
For the body was destined for things that were
Far more subtle. Anything could happen
With such a body. A prey to pink
Make-up. To moments of stillness and calm.
And to successful imitations of the mouth.

First of all to take a shower; to see to it
That she take a shower.
To brush my teeth. To see to it
That she brush her teeth.
For what the words said
Did not come out of the words.

To follow gulls in the movement of the waves.
To become writing, even seen from far away,
To accompany each word with the thing that splits it,
And not only with its own silence.
To accompany each word with what it doesn't say
Enough, with what, in itself, distracts it from the meaning
It proclaims. With what cancels it out.

Under the poppies, the field,
Covered with red earth, entirely
Red; the sumptuousness of this color.

*

Farther off, the green sumptuousness of the grass.

To calm down, to keep the rhythm; to see to it
That she keep the rhythm.

*

The red color of the poppies
Was not the color red, it was
The color of the poppies.

The sea was a piece of earth. The bedroom
Was a city, intermingling the smells
Of grass and of flowers. – The flowers
Changed colors. – To see now only
The light, the simulation of that disturbing
Thing that would have to be disposed of,
In the unusual cutting up of familiar
Poses.

In Alexandria, in the bedroom with closed shutters,
Scarcely lit by the light bulb of a lamp,
In search of an impure elegance,
Of a handkerchief, a slightly heavy eyelid,
A rapid assiduity; far from the pleasures
Known by intelligence and by the torments
Of History, with the possession that came
From the alleys, boutiques and bars,
And this light, soothing, murmured bond,
In the deep softness of uncertainty
And admission, the provisional imperfection
And the material quality of bodies,
Constantin Pierre Cavafy.

What crossed the image also crossed your gaze.
Reassessment, found object. – It was a world
In which there was nothing to see. – Pure emotion.
Leaning on a solitude that it was unaware of.
You shared a fragment of this emotion with me.
From which nothing was lacking.

Such was the logic of verse. To slow the sentence
Down. Everything that was on the ground. Abandoned
Fictions. Tiny sounds that the street left
On the façades. What the gaze lacked.
The difference between man and woman. Turtledove
Gray. Warm brown. Disparities provoked
By walking. Gray or green tufts of grasses.
Banks of accumulated dusts. What you said.
What I said. Feigned loves. Obscure words
Archaically pronounced. And spit too.
The episodic sister. Necessary penetrations.
Certain odors that I could not recognize.
And pushing your tongue back.

*

Silliness, affective stupidity.

Not to forget the image of Trèves, on the wall, in a corner,
The effigy of the wine boat, with its casks
And vine-growers. – The jasmine from elsewhere,
The walls of the Roman city. – Not to forget
That sleep was a living matter.
Not to forget to watch the figure
Of one's body.

To say nothing. – Not to get tense.
Not to shout. – To retain that something
In you. – To slip. – To slip beneath me.
Slowly, hardly, toward the left side.
To give ourselves time. No softness.
To lose nothing of this light color.
No pleasure, no tenderness.

*

Outside, the window outlined
The blue mass of a rainy season.

To sleep. – To hide that mobility of the words
That drove you crazy. – Head buried
In the cave that you dug
To shelter your fingers.

*

The green color of the grass was not
The color green, it was the color of the grass.

To like flowers. – Dried flowers.
Talismen, the moist color of bodies,
Sweat, bogeymen. – To like the color
Of flowers, the ashen color left
On the corner of your lips. – And to refuse to shout.

The inability to make love
In this dead language. – The inability
To run in this dress any more.
With the blue of your body, at shoulder
Height, the remarkable complicity
Of blue. – and before the eddies of the river,
That first winter, wanting to give a meaning
To that new landscape.

You thought that the image came from somewhere else,
The image came from the arrangement of the poem,
From the idea we had of the poem,
From the arrangement of the poem or from the absence
Of order in the arrangement of the poem or
From the absence in the order of the poem.
You thought that the image of the mouth
Was an excessive image. – Your hand
Was still touching me. I prepared myself
To think that the night would not end.

Several winds banked toward the west.
Night was ending. I recognized
What remained of the night. – What remained,
The bare face, the blatancy of the shoulder.
And something else I forgot.

The taste of not telling only the truth.

Words crashed to the ground.
They preserved the taste of an apparent light.
The taste of a transitional exactitude. The taste,
And the memory, of the calculation of chimera.

After so many objects, a self-imposed silence.
To stop at the entrance of the body. To preserve
The smell of the linen. To descend. To try
To talk, a little more. To try to believe
The lightness, the derisiveness, voluptuousness,
Abuse, exist; and to caress your lips.

Something immobile and stifling in the air.
A single window, a single lamp. The curve of the eyes,
The coiling of the forearm. The coarseness of the ultimate
Delicacy.

*

You began to laugh, the laugh choked
Into a groan, you began to cry.

No, it was not an ordinary day.
Smells rose. Night rose.
Your voice rose. You spoke. It was
A difficult language.

*

You tried to dream of something else.
You tried not to see me anymore.

I didn't dare ask you to walk slower.

You sought the truth. – And the voracity,
That was not forgotten.

PORCELAIN BLUE, ROYAL BLUE

A few prose scraps confronted one another.
Nothing superfluous. – The organic stripping down
Of the sentence. – A summer sun, in the middle of winter
Very cold. – I was far from the birds of your garden,
And from the lids of your eyes.

*

And that silence, that no body
Had ever given.

You stayed still. What detached itself
From you stayed still. We no longer went out.
The sounds, near you, stayed still.
The words, flashes, sweat, desire, stayed
Still. – The moving of the sounds. – The obstacle
Of the words. – The extremity of the flash. – The work
Of the sweat. – The finesse of desire. – The very
Products of stillness, stayed still.
Stillness was what we assumed had been acquired.
Which continued.

To be in the cold. To be naked. To watch
The evening rise, in the color that came
From the sky, and also from the ground, from the houses.
To watch the words become silent
Speech. To watch what you were watching.
A gull or red-breast, or the reflection
Of a gull.

You were still more naked than I.
You dressed, you undressed
In a certain way. – You tried
To make me believe that that wasn't
Important, that it didn't come from that.

*

That everything could come out of the body.

That there was silence.

*

And something else.

The ability, in the bedroom,
    Curtains drawn,
To push back the late hour,
The memory you still had
Of what had happened,
    There, yesterday,
Or else, to wait until tomorrow.

*

You had a rather vast body,
    Rather solid,
    A definitive body.

There was the identification of what we said
With the constraints of the poem, with the shaping
Of the constraints of the poem, with the consistency of the verb,
So many hours spent with no object other than the landscape,
Stationary or mobile, with no object other than the description
Of the landscape, in the disorder and the artfulness of an animal
Matter.

*

And nothing to say, beyond a single word.

The Portrait was not a portrait
With a great table covered with fruit
Of the season, or with fine
Vegetables, a freshly-sliced loaf of bread,
The favor of origins, the appetite for violence,
Or hiding out in the sexual uproar.

*

It didn't turn black.

To eat chicken in Prague, and fresh
Lettuce hearts, in the steady light
Of the façades and the grace of the walls, accompanied
By mild desires and virtues, in the inability
To satisfy the very idea of happiness;
With the temporal softness that prepared
And multiplied it, that well-being, at times,
And nothing to say, augmenting
It with nothing to say.

Or else to throw up, you said.

*

Or else to refuse to throw up.

Steeped in a completely fabricated tradition,
Regulated by strange laws, with prohibitive details,
Inappropriate customs, misgivings,
Lies that knew what they owed
To sad outbursts. – Murders.
The exercise of ambitions. – A writing
In search of loose living. – Even ingenuity,
Even a faulty one, that could tear a little life
Out of this bleeding prey. There was no
Other truth.

*

That's how the sentence could have begun.
With the Portrait.

Portugal, Praia de Vieira,
Where the fog, at the bottom of the sea,
Passed under the gulls.
While the sun beat
Down on the limestone
Of the rocks and the light
Remained between the sea and
The seashore.

*

The slow rising toward the windows,
The night.

Among the numerous colors (carmine, orange
Dead leaves, porcelain blue and royal blue,
Oyster shell, gardenia, light brown and dust,
Teak, ash and vermilion…), behind the window,
A huge unknown bird observed us.
That's what could give the poem
Some quality. What you would have said. What was
Impossible.

Peire Cardenal,

Martim Codax, Hadewijch d'Anvers, Auzias March,

Camoëns, Adrian

Roland Holst, Marina Tsvetaeva, Fernando Pessoa,

Mina Loy, the Italians,

The Germans, the Americans, František Halas,

Vladimir Holan, Laco

Novomesky, Jaroslav Seifert, Alexander Tvardovsky,

Bert Schierbeek, Lucebert,

The Dutch poets of the fifties,

Yolanda Pantin, Adília

Lopes, the tangos, fados, sonnets…

The hundred-year-old troubadour, the Galego-Portuguese,
The Flemish beguine, the lord,
The adventurer, the poet poet, the love woman,
The alcoholic of Lisbon, Cravan's wife,
The three Czechs, the Slovak, the Soviet journal
Editor, Bert Schierbeek, Lucebert,
The Caracas beauty, and the woman that lived
On the road of dead lands.

At times, another's word
Was painful (or pretended
To be), and the sun, every day,
Became whiter.

*

You looked at the evening.

To dream was inevitable. – It was necessary
To maintain the dream, and the scar of the dream,
And the walk toward the shadow in the city
Where you were born. Very near by, in an undeserving
Alley.

That was not a dream. I never dreamed.
That was not a dream that I could have
Dreamt. It was a conversation with
Words, a simple conversation.

*

With tenuous moods,
For fertile constraints.

The city crumbled into dust.
You thought you could enter
Death, get used to the idea
Of death, that you could fill out
The poem, that the conversation could
Stop there, that the dream was what remained
Of fate, the variation, the symmetry, of a slow surprise.
You walked with your corpse.

Very near by, in an undeserving alley,
A little girl hesitated to enter a bar.

The story was fabulous.
Fabulous was the story.
Only the fragment was illusory.

*

It was brief.

To keep still and silent.
Obsessed by stillness and silence.
To exist in a sort of eternity
That was not that of the sentences
That I repeated, and that were added
To the gilded half-light. To attempt, humbly,
To dream.

*

And the silence, that came from you.

The others died.

Dying was a custom
Before dreaming of children,

Of the unfortunate effigy
Of unfortunate children,

Of the rough-hewn rock
Idol, of heavy clothes,

Of the sacrifice of horses and men,
Of the death of women, of the death

Of prisoners, of the death of dogs,
Of everything that dies in the smell

Of sulfur and infamy.

What you said preserved
A flavor of disgrace, the charm,
The perpetual humiliation of the poem.
Which never happened. Which
Remained in the words.

*

For what happened one time
Happened another time, which
Wasn't even another time.

To be born near the sea and a clay pigeon.
To spend one's time transporting water,
In a fake pitcher, of fake blue porcelain.
Not managing to cross the street.

*

It was a city with one entrance and one exit.

You liked the hotels, the hostels,
The inns, the rooms rented by the hour,
The insolent ornament of the walls. The stillness
Of the boats on the stillness of the sea.

*

And that obligation to attain clarity.

We visited museums, at random
As we passed through somewhat secluded cities,
Of little interest, little museums,
Of local glories and a few beautiful
Things never seen before; and also a few
Large works, few paintings,
Where you had to seek out the anecdote,
Then count the number of fruit.

Daylight mixed its shadow with one last image.
It touched the infinity of last images.
It touched the infinity of barren lands.

*

It mixed its shadow with that
Of barrens.

And, near your naked body, the stillness
Of boats on the sea.

The situation, which was not recounted.
A great stain of light, which
Exhausted itself in duration, the wheel,
Which turned, near the bridge, and
The Portrait, near the naked body.

Because the truth was useless, because
The truth of the poem was in the poem,
And only there, because nostalgia
Was a useless prose, it was necessary
To isolate verse, isolate its story
And say what we had to say.

Rhythm could not be outside verse.

Form was elementary. Form
And color. Color was
Elementary. Because it was necessary not
To fear repetition, the words
Hardly touched what they could
Touch. Because the poem was a useless prose.

To avoid decoration and lyricism,
To avoid lyricism and pure decoration,
To avoid decoration and pure lyricism.
To move toward a more compact,
Less eloquent, more analytical localization. Less
Conventions, even popular ones. More
Episodes, approaches. Less formulas.
More observations.

*

Not to talk about one's life.

You said it was false. Really false.
You could live without obscenity; words
Didn't scare you. But it was
The comfortable respect of the poem
That won out. – You wrote:
Take me in your mouth, and you thought:
Suck me.

Herons, then, filled the bed.
Herons fell.
Herons with steel-blue talons.

Henri Deluy

Born in 1931, Henri Deluy began his career as a teacher, journalist, and librarian. Since 1954, he has edited the influential poetic journal *Action poétique.* Among his many books of poetry are *Les Mille* (1980); *La Substitution* (1983); *Vingt-quatre heures d'amour en juillet, puis en août; Premières suites* (1987), and *La Répétition autrement la Différence* (1992). *L'amour charnel* (*Carnal Love*) was published in 1994. He has also edited several anthologies and translated the work of Fernando Pessoa, Alexandre Tvardovsky, Jaroslav Seifert, Constantin Cavafy and others.

SUN & MOON CLASSICS